Copyright 2019 Amber Rae Johnson

This book is not intended as a substitute for the medical advice of physicians. The reader should regularly consult a physician in matters relating to his/her health and particularly with respect to any symptoms that may require diagnosis or medical attention.

Urth Publishing
ISBN: 978-0-578-22507-4

Written by Amber Rae Johnson
Illustrations by Felipe dos Reis Chaves
Contributions by Tayler Wooten

This is a work of fiction. Names, characters, businesses, places, events, locales, and incidents are either the products of the author's imagination or used in a fictitious manner. Any resemblance to actual persons, living or dead, or actual events is purely coincidental.

Big Questions Book Series

First Printing in 2019

All rights reserved. This book or any portion of it may not be reproduced or used in any manner whatsoever without the express written permission of the publisher except for the use of brief quotations in a book review.

For my beautiful son, Maze, the miracle that inspired this series.
May you always show love and kindness, even when faced with adversity.

Maze and Baloo are curious boys, thinking and thinking when they play with their toys.

When they have big questions they know what to do, they ask someone smart to find out what's true.

What are Vaccines?

WRITTEN BY
AMBER RAE JOHNSON

"What are vaccines?" asked Maze, out of the blue.

"They're available to everyone, even your teeny tiny kitten."

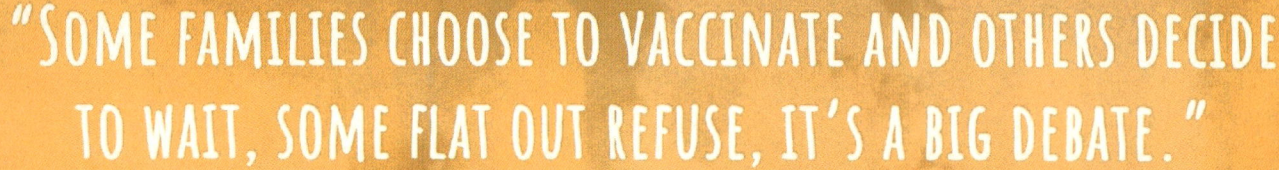

"Some families choose to vaccinate and others decide to wait, some flat out refuse, it's a big debate."

"Should they be friends with me?
What if they act scared?
Can I give them illnesses?
Will they think that I'm impaired?"

"You can not spread an illness that you've never had, so be happy and well and nobody should be mad."

Made in the USA
San Bernardino, CA
11 March 2020